Paradise Stairway

Glen Cavaliero.
Cambridge
1980

Glen Cavaliero

Paradise Stairway

CARCANET/MANCHESTER

IN MEMORY OF MY FATHER AND MOTHER

Acknowledgements are due to the editors of the following magazines, in which some of these poems originally appeared: *The Cambridge Review, Delta, In Particular, New Poetry I, New Poetry II* (Arts Council), *New Poetry* (Workshop Press), *The New Yorker, Omens, Ostrich, Poetry Nation* and *Stand*.

SBN 85635 223 3
Copyright © Glen Cavaliero 1977

All rights reserved

First published in 1977
by Carcanet New Press Limited
330 Corn Exchange
Manchester M4 3BG

Printed in Great Britain by
Unwin Brothers Limited, Old Woking

The publishers acknowledge the financial assistance of the
Arts Council of Great Britain.

CONTENTS

Retreat to Moscow / 7
Prevention / 9
At Pleshey / 10
The Grave Unseen / 11
Pennine Chapel / 13
The Tarn / 14
Poor Old Thing / 16
Pettifeet / 17
Beauty Spot / 19
Staffs / 20
White Rose City / 21
Caretaker / 23
Paradise Stairway / 25
Deposition / 26
Under Pendle Hill / 27
Dozmary Pool / 29
The Old Track / 31
Morning Country / 32
Escape / 33
Anchorite / 34
A Redundant Church / 35
Somersby / 36
Hollywood the Golden / 37
Veronica / 39
Master and Servant / 40
The Maids of Le Mans / 41
Big Baby / 42
At the Spa / 43
Doddynell / 44
Wet Sleddale: On Good Friday / 45
In the Gardens: Villa Cimbrone / 47
The Brink / 49
Priested Shore / 50
Ruined / 51
The Disposal of the Dead / 52
Mine / 54

RETREAT TO MOSCOW

Do you want to be your self,
    that mature man of myth?
        Then listen carefully to the poem:
            it will show you the way.

Taking your thickest coat,
    boots and a warm hat,
        and not forgetting your gloves
            (for it will be very cold

in the place where you are going)
    you must turn right about:
        next, armoured and unblinking,
            walk into your own mind

where a whole Russia of snows
    awaits your coming—
        league upon league of loneliness:
            so watch yourself depart

as the poem moves on
    (your only possible weapon)
        and diminishing before you
            plods that determined manikin

who, as he goes, talks,
    just as my pen moves now,
        talks to himself, still reasoning
            in quizzical desperation

against the perpetual denial
    that this flight was free,
        that the clothes are clothing
            and not a straitjacket.

You can still see yourself?
    Then you must keep moving:
        unthinkable to stop now,
            for snows here are quagmires

into which you never know
    the mercy of quite sinking;
        and beware of saboteurs
            within and without, unseen

but whispering; be resolved
    that you are not afraid
        and will thus never despair.
            Do you understand that?

Go on then further
    into your own shadow
        till the only thing that remains
            is a mere speck vibrating,

vanishing out of sight,
    out of your sight anyway:
        now you must be blind,
            deaf, dumb if possible,

avoiding needless movement
    until the traveller returns
        bringing what you already know
            but do not know as yet

because you are not your self
    until the messenger returns
        bringing what you asked for,
            what you wanted to know—remember?

Till then you will never know
    whether what it travels to
        is something worse than extinction—
            the knowledge of its final error;

or whether at the limit of the mind
    it will walk, clad so warmly,
        out of its shadow into
            the ironic sanction of the sun.

PREVENTION

The project was my own transport
to such a place; to follow
and for exercise, the climb—

that stiff, rough lane
which reaches, on the other side,
history, a museum of images,

the dream. Now that I'm over
the abbey gate's the barrier,
having scaled the hill to meet me:

I had recalled this little
city wrong way round.
In a quiet Mass at dawn

I blend with waiting women
round a stone where time accumulates
the space I've learned to breathe in.

Orare, laborare . . .
That interruption over,
the workmen's hands proved friendly.

And after, I was where I was,
I thought, about to be
till it seemed that time was lost

I must return to find.
An old blind nun
hands back my watch

no longer as I'd left it;
the dial is squared with jewels
in a way I never wanted.

Who's taken up my time?
Henceforth it's downhill back,
back every inch till waking.

AT PLESHEY

Wood that was hacked to make Good Easter steeple
fenced-in a homestead

domestic and combustible,
one in substance with the wood of woods at Waltham

Holy Cross, palings at Leaden Roding
and the Blackmore belfry.

But the stockades have collapsed:
rats splash about in the ditches of damp Pleshey

where the calm lips of Anglicans compassionate the Mysteries—
defence with a difference.

I am encountered:
an angry emptiness goes lumbering round the church.

What has afflicted me? The spitting witches of Essex?
That dove-shit on the floor?

Anger! Anger!
Defence is a fraud. There was no war, ever.

Tall birches of Hatfield, oaks of Ongar,
green and silver,

embroider the chasuble
of Cedd, guardian of the last sanctuary. When

am I my own? In a where only. But not here,
not in these woods I blacken.

THE GRAVE UNSEEN

He is alone
bemused
at the track's end
worn out by thought
and daylong searching
deaf from the tune
of the wind and thundering
water's cry

old men on the moor
have led him downward
abandoned him
by the headstrong flood
whose foam wrenched round
consorted boulders
cannons down the gorge
in a ball of noise

the air's a wall
the beck's explosion
resonant
hollows a quietness
void within void
within vapourized
rock and bracken
womb of the word

called up through a voice
neither present nor previous
though all-but-now
like the rustle of furze
sound within sound
as if from some miner
drowned in the rending
dam upstream

a decoy cry
in the wet light

that moves about him
a pliant ghost
by the broken footbridge
slimy with spray
offering the leaper
an unplumbed fall

a place of sadness
insupportable
a rusted winch
but never a tomb
an abandonment
a quest defeated
by force of gravity's
long way home

PENNINE CHAPEL

Brick bawler glares
with pounded fist, slammed doors;

gravestones on end like hair,
cash-weighted, tilt in terror

while grit on the louder wind
spits up the valley floor

to crown each sainted slab
like pity, blackening the lot.

THE TARN

    The Lakeland writers patronize it
striding by in their big boots on the way to Walna Scar.
'A small reedy pool'—so Wainwright, correct as always:
it's not really a tarn at all, you can pass it without knowing,
  and it's fast vanishing among the rushes. 'Boo Tarn'—
    the very name sounds foolish, especially for
'the smallest in the district' (Baddeley), even though
the original name was Booth Tarn (Heaton Cooper)
    'from the Norse *budhar*, meaning hut.'
    Evidently someone lived there once.

    Someone lived there, an unknown mind
would watch the light opened outwards over the bay at dawn
held high at noon until scratched out by the night's thrusting
                                                      cone
(the tarn's burnished surface its record, clear and open then
  before the reeds got hold) and up in the cove by Goatswater
  would hear the foxes bark and the sheep's thin cry
  spread the alarm as the quiet and nameless men
scattering on the moor below were butchered by the
                                                      Norsemen.
    Budhar, a hut: for all its mild nonentity
  the place has a past, was born in blood.

    The wind too, just there, is a killer.
It blows so hard, with a sudden vicious whip it can send you
                                                    sprawling,
and the rocks around are enough to break your fall, and you
                                                      with it,
on this harsh highway where the walkers stumble, misled into
                                                  the quarries.
Somehow it's less peaceful here than you might expect.
  The place calls for attention, stays in the mind
  with a kind of stubbornness. Is it because of the name,
or because of some thing that precedes the name, an ancient
                                                    presence
    known to the ravens in the rocks, coeval
    with the ferns and flooding stream,

       a presence that compelled a name? All
who come here both give and receive the name. Stand on the
                                                                   ledge
that tilts to hold the tarn in place, and let the water well
up into your eyes' liberty. The surface strains through reeds
  to reveal its true extent, its shape, to you
    the lord, the namer: you will not forget what you see,
    for it is what you have chosen to see. Then the reeds'
persistent wavering blurs your vision; you wait in doubt
    a moment longer, loath to move
      and feeling, when you do, deprived, bereaved.

      Boo Tarn: or any tarn,
or any place, gate, coppice or fence that strikes the eye,
it's the same thing always: stay long enough and you start to
                                                                    grow
into your five-fold elemental-rooted body where
  budhar, a hut or booth, is still sufficient
    cause of sight, a sign that as the tarn is swung
    round on its vast, exposed, determined course,
its waters held in place by the earth's indrawn breath,
    this small reedy pool
      transmits a planetary light.

POOR OLD THING

She venerates the Virgin, her face a scored page,
relic of a long game of noughts and crosses.

Wound up, her voice rotates on grievances
(but always general, national, not particular.)

Limp as the thin blue woollens hanging
year by year in her great-aunt's tallboy,

she smells bad, sadly; loves the Lord,
hammering nails of kindness all around her.

She has never once done a dishonest deed
in a stifled lifetime of dishonest breathing.

And she is lonely, living with a sickness past all cure.

I wonder: has she ever imagined you
uncurled beside me in such yearning nakedness?

And could she dream of gently rocking curtains
and the harbour sounds? this scorching stroke of sun?

PETTIFEET

My name is Pettifeet.
Under my cloche
my fringe is grey
and my eyes are grey
on each side of my nose,
the little bird nose
my lovers were proud of
you liked to assume.
My skirts are too short
but my coat is swathed tight;
the smart shoes
at the ends of my legs
have brave shiny buckles—
a quaint little dame
from the mid-nineteen-twenties
preserved for a decade
to walk in your mind.
You guessed all about me,
suspected a poverty
of cash and companionship,
christened me Pettifeet
('You can see that she's proud
of those poor little legs')
and watched me grow older
('She's breaking up quickly')
and then disappear
on a single phrase spoken
surprisingly deep
when at last overheard:
'I was really ast*oun*ded!'

By what or by whom?
The voice wasn't Pettifeet's:
it belonged to the body
(Mrs Groom? Miss Maguire?)
who owned all the clothes
and the eyes and the feet
and the debonair legs,

who was quite unaware
of Pettifeet legends,
who died long ago
taking Pettifeet with her

until today
at a pause on the corner
a grey pair of eyes
and a tight-folded hat
raise a red folded coat,
a precarious walk
and a ghost of such poignance,
of such utter absence,
shadowed, unending
without a beginning
and bringing back with her
the one who had noticed
the lie of the legs
and concocted the story,
the one who is dead,
who was loved and is dead,
who alone understood
the mystery of Pettifeet,
who like Miss Maguire
(or like Mrs Groom?)
vanished, gone under,
turns up in the person
of Pettifeet smiling
in charming exchange.

What ghost of which woman
I almost remember
will never be known,
but your ghost is amused,
I would guess, to be linked with
that delicate totter,
content to come back
(how else on this morning?)
through a bright pair of eyes
under Pettifeet's hat.

BEAUTY SPOT

    The angels were insistent:
        not there—here;
for the third time they carted stones
    to the mound beside the stream,

    and surely with a view
        to the future: painters
year in, year out,
    lived off the broad spire

    shingled above the cross,
        whose imaginary directives
from aloft hallowed the blackened timbers
    reeking of high tea

    as the quiet mud-river
        slipped by willows
loop after loop across the marsh
    to select family beaches,

    and the brash departing coaches
        lumbered hooting
through the long elm tunnel, salt
    breezes crushed in carbon.

    From the neat burial mound
        a belle madonna
gentlewoman, Bloomsbury-bred,
    attests divine civility,

    stoops to the angel: so
        God's colony
is settled here upon the chalk
    beyond all bungalows:

    the tourists think it's lovely.
        They are right: the downs
are a heavenly prospect of repose
    from every budding site.

STAFFS

    Cement dust upon the hedges
and in each scruffy town a hold-up at the crossing:
the Roaches, black and fearsome, become delectable
    mountains I cannot reach
    for the smoking vents before me.
Highways like sellotape strap up this country
whose charred red brick and green canals
    have got into my head
    stuffed tight enough to burst:
the Give Way signs rear up at every junction.
From Tamworth through Tutbury to Cheadle I have
                                    laboured, and all
    the houses were blockaded by No Parking.
    There were dead children on Cannock,
stately Victorian Gothic at Hoar Cross,
and I have knelt at the feet of Chad, in Penda's kingdom
    left uncomforted: at Stowe
    Pool I was not baptized.
Drab Staffordshire, you correlate my soul,
obscured county. When shall I find your upright
    sanctuaries? or know their God?

WHITE ROSE CITY

The stone lace lantern
burns no longer;
Galtres' murderous glades
are hacked; no corpses
hang from the fat keep
where Robert Aske
was tossed in his iron suit
from hell to heaven;
and you can drive a Bentley
slap through
the gates where skulls have dried
to strengthen law.
But though the city breaks
its silver belt
those ramparts still restrict it
to a ballad past
from which it profits, flush
with faiths and wars.

When Rome had carved the North
with ramrod roads,
the turncoat Saxons set
the steeples growing
up to the High God,
outsoaring law
on the wings of hewn rock,
with leaded eyes
smoke-blue and emerald
and the medieval
tawny-rusted gold.
Prayer stopped
all traffic for a while,
till the minster crumbled:
now the saints are housed
in a few sad
old Anglo-Catholic junkshops—
all lace and tat.

Such fragile queens and martyrs
stare at dirt,
fit targets for a football;
and the streams
of prayer are left to silt,
for long ago
the brutal Danish raiders
scrapped all
nonsense of that kind.
In Skeldersgate,
in Shambles, brass clattered:
watch how
at night on Coney Street
the dandy boys
and bandbox girls in pawn
reflect the goods,
and under shredding pinnacles
roar up the town.

White rose city,
old as the time
it takes to grow from law
through frantic faith
to a slow death from plenty;
city of thorns,
old as the hungry woods,
the chopped-up bodies
and the bitter grip of winter:
you have known
the scourge that whips to frenzy;
stench of streets;
and the thick oily flood
of tidal years—
and are our city:
your walls, our banished ghosts;
your shops, our arteries;
your towers, all we have lost.

CARETAKER

The sodden snow rings melancholy chords upon his mind,
a kind of soft-shoe shuffle for a migrant hoofer
to perform against the downbeat of each drumming truck.
Slush guttering from eaves in the Old Town
curdles each stagnant pond to milk
up on the shuttered Public Library's concrete lid.
The locked glass shop doors snub like broken promises,
and in St Edmund, King and Martyr,
the Reverend Everard Wilson, B.A. Leeds,
expounds the book of Daniel to a few
beneath old sagging boards.
      The night is caving in
      on the linked young
      strollers glumly
      fused in a perpetual
      post-coital *tristesse*.

From dreams of tumult he still feels his throat constrict at
                                          the thought
of a gloved hand upon his choker, still shivers at the cold
sound of the Red Guards loose among the exhibits—
pallid statuary of a civilization's sabbath
poised for the smash-up . . . And he sees the dowsers
stalk, back and forth, their sharp hands hooked
around the trembling twig: they know the floods are pushing
                                                  upward.
Snow slipped unsuspected down
last night and dripped through to his bedroom ceiling;
next there'll be a sharp rap at the door
and debris piled in the streets—
      alarm clocks, ledgers, spectacles,
      old manuscripts,
      his teapot, dentures
      and the other requirements
      all prised out. Those odds have gone.

He has heard that far away in the forest in a place concealed
                                                  from view

is a huge pullulating dump where strange births occur:
bred from battery birds, eggs 'consigned as surplus'
in reversion rot unsold; but not unsought.
Small beaks chirp wide open,
fatherless; soft feathers needing Bedlam light
scramble out of the stench, hop for a while, to be then
                                                            crunched
by the rat hoards that scratch and slide
across the grimy shells, as thick as lice,
a heaving stew of fur in constant motion:
he hears them all night long . . .
    A bobby shines a torch,
    gives him a frown;
    the wind's savage
    and his shoes are soaked.
    A young guardsman stares him down.

PARADISE STAIRWAY

Beneath the Trinity
John Keats, junketing
before he coughed up blood,
cast out a cauliflower,
one fowl, some macaroni
and a poor rice pudding—
keeping the plates, but gesturing
against bad food, bad diet
and all such sloppy cooking.
It had been a lifetime's work.

Sleep and poetry:
the two don't go together.
The athletic medico
sped after laurels
four thousand lines around the moon,
breathless set out to climb
rungs to the sun: the way was blocked.
The end was Rome and a few odes,
and when at last he reached
the Trinity his lungs were gone.

Sung out:
diminishing applause
was all he heard . . . Useless
and hackneyed as a faded rose
an ageing Broadway actress throws
her latchkey down
to the lurking mercenary crotch,
falls back, awaits her lay
long and hopeless as the dying
poet's clutch on day.

Such steps
are climbed or else they throw you.
Christ keeps open house
at the top: in the back garden
Princess Napoleon (nude by Canova)

eyes men up and down.
Like golden cypresses the candles
steady behind shut doors
for every youthful poet dead
and all live whores.

DEPOSITION

In the gale, on the moor,
an immense creaking—
a weight as of an imponderable
burden, something improbable
as the upending of the mountain
on which we tottered, drenched near nightfall.

And then we saw it.
Thrusting at the buffets
of that black wind, we stormed upwards
as it lurched to meet us
weighed down it seemed
not by the air but by the hanging man.

You'd have thought he was hurrying,
nailed though he was,
to greet us. But he fell
face down as the cross fell,
splayed out on the mud
in the ooze and horse-droppings and the mark of trampling
                                                                  feet.

We felt we must bury him;
the bones were heavy
but the ground was soft, it was soon over.
So that was the end of it.
It's odd we could have thought
he was coming to meet us. Love dies hard.

UNDER PENDLE HILL

for John and Anne Lee

witches are frequent—on pub signs,
on tea-room doors and posters,
garden gates; they're fitted out
with steeple hats, long spindly brooms
and a prim puss that's no way like
the real gripe-clawed grimalkin.
Night sweat's been exorcized—
old terrors have their uses; but the hill
has power to raise them still,
black in all weathers from afar
and resonant among the valleys
of a dim name few women can remember.

That long swart shoulder
would tempt any wench
pent up in Sabden or in Barley
to ride on Satan's gusty stallion
right up to the crest. But no
wind from the west can blow away
their torment only younger than the hill—
small wonder, then or now, that broth grew black,
cows slipped their young
and children disappeared. Gaunt
from their lust, these women crept
their way through whispers to the branding flame

in twisted martyrdom. A few
bold rag-bag men,
two ancient grannies, blind and poor,
and a host of kin and rumours led
a whole duchy by the ears,
and fooled its wise and Christian king
to their own undoing. Such backward chimes
were tolled spite flourished like a nettle,
broke out in boils and scabs;
a starved nag and yawning belly

trod the air, to knock
on walls at midnight and to cripple sleep.

No quaintness here—a bent desire:
and still on the grave moor,
gazing out across the stacks,
one starts to shape the furtive wraith
of some old Chattox gathering herbs,
alone with her own devil . . . Smoke
is rising over Nelson, over Colne,
above the grizzled brick and cobble stairs
that claw the slopes. The rain pours grime; the hardy houses,
terrace on terrace, scoured
and cleanly, grin defiance at the mirk.

Spawned by the slack mills, and spurned,
their folk might seem to breed
on Demdike soil. Bleak Lancashire
here meets its own mirage—
neat counterpart of fields
easing out of the bell heather,
all swept by rain, the hills free
and the beck undammed. Brick chokes the clough,
and dirtied words abuse
the yards and alleys; but the farms shine
high on the glistening green
below the purple summits in the morning,

and anger turns to eagerness:
the devil's duped. Crammed
abundant shop fronts bulge and prams
are huge with young. No sterile power
of boss or warlock can withstand
the spell of plenty; mockery
in store and stadium, fog and flood,
allays old hatreds, bells the town.
Bury the old books:
up under Pendle, parked beside
the Rough Lee walls, unpacked
encampments leave a wicked litter for the wind.

DOZMARY POOL

for Mary Walder

A strained light as of steel:
   is it the sword's flight
      that colours all
this day, this moor, this utmost weather?
   Or the whiteness of an arm
     from the deep, the brandisher?
      The utterance of gulls'
blunt sight of earth and ocean
   is borne on the dulled iron
     wind swishing the lake
      against the sedges
savaged by the ruts of tractor tyres.

   A bottomless mere, the cause
     thick grasping ooze
      and someone drowned,
the body never to be recovered:
   this then the cradle
     of holy Arthur's passing?
      Rain spits
on the slant air across the tors,
   and the holiday traffic jollies
     past the Jamaica Inn
      where signs with care
direct one to Brown Willy and the Pool.

   I stood on Brown Willy
     yesterday: territory
      only for the shaggy
cattle below me, but on the summit
   the mark of horses' hooves.
     One of Mordred's ministers?
      Or Merlin? Bors?
An over-obvious poetry, rather
   some jogging Jill or Jennifer.
     But comfortable afternoon

  smoothed all
doubts. And the stonechats sounded friendly.

  This morning's air
  prolongs the lack of mood;
   visitors arrive
in a Rover to view the haunted pool
  as I have come, as you,
  with an imposition of legends—
   the Sword, the Mere,
the Death of the Last King, the Wailing—
  conjuring an overworld
  of underworld remembering,
   indigenous magic,
our native dialogue with space.

  On a far skyline, spectral,
  the clay cones of St Austell
   gatecrash the colloquy—
anachronistic witch-hills
  with the tantalization of the abandoned
  shafts and engine houses,
   reliquary chasms
where we dropped a pebble bounding into quiet:
  bottomless indeed!
  No cob's creature
   stirred in the dark
at the summons of that idle sounding.

  And now the flat comfortable
  quilting of the pool's surface
   cries us quits,
gusts in the grass and the temperate contours
  of the mild moor in summer
  wrap up our unease.
   The valley slips
down to the sea and a midday meal;
  next comes St Neot with the angels,
  and the Devil's Cheesewring, then
   with luck
the Smuggler's Arms will deliver a cream tea.

THE OLD TRACK

Not a gust stirs the thicket, and the mud
   has split wide open.
      A rabbit lollops

through the sharp green wheat, vagabond.
   What am I doing here?
      Not wanted

now, any such questions,
   for dust is breath. The track
      draws on

with never a gate, ignores all bridle paths,
   the Iron Age earthwork,
      lovers in the spinney.

To sprawl upon a bramble bank to choose
   my way leads nowhere
      under speedwell skies.

There's a humming in the briars, the larks are ceaseless.
   What the ghost road is
      I am—

a link, a shaping of recurrence. Elsewhere
   and nowhere I take it with me,
      death or life.

MORNING COUNTRY

for Paul Townsend

    I have strayed into a landscape without frontiers
below a Grecian sky. These buckler cliffs
    are no horizon; alien, they suggest
    Monument Valley, and World's End
as a name does not mislead: it spells a freedom
    from the too close here of now.

    For this is morning country.
I have seen it, the summit brandishing a hold
    ruined past what can be remembered,
    and the deep cwm with the foxgloves
where the warren is, squat thorns and tumbled rocks.
    I breathe its inmost air

    while memory envelops colour:
the pallid moor-grass; young uncurling fronds
    of lime-green bracken, flawless at the point
    of drought; the wild geranium's purple
and the slender horses cantering with their foals in light
    I had not learned to see

    in earlier vision. But the dawn
came up today in double light upon
    the land where I have walked continually
    to show it timeless in this backward lane
that quivers in the heat. The hills roll westward
    out of slumber, and I wake

    on warm brown grass,
my breath adhering to the pace of the briar's growth
    beside the wall, that homely garth
    I do not fear to leave behind me,
for no traveller remains in morning country; death
    paves all those hills with gold.

ESCAPE

The moorland breeze, delicate with heather,
bubbles in a well of curlews;
their reckless beaks are scimitars
that pierce each gust.

Who'd scent the Lamb of God?
My fear coils up asleep,
an adder in a bilberry clump.

A far-off smudge of wool
rots on the bank where shooting-butts
creak like extorted joints
of prisoners shovelled under
living and forgotten.

The flocks are deep in fold.

Foreclosing light lays bronze
on Llantysilio Mountain, and the wind
picks at that sullied fleece.

ANCHORITE

The convenience of a squint
for the eye bent
on where the angels are is obvious;
how from the slant aisle
hands that count the event
leave free the eye, the rover,
to slip through stone,
air and again stone,
to hands, both same and other,
raising host-high the Host
to Its source where all is over.

Up a rustification of ladders
gaunt weight
can tread the years down hard, beseeching
eyes blurred with the small speckled man
dropped on his dam's knee,
pitted with penury and clothed
in too-late arms,
a body of rubbish
littering the world in gloom, and starving
year upon lean year
in that despair investing.

An obsession with the doom-
laden shoulderer of all souls
who appeals with a gambler's hand
to the magisterial eye on nerves of flame
is narrowed to the cell's energy—
the daily muttering
of the toll exacted,
the bread, the prattle of the birds,
the rank privy and, on occasion,
in the chequered Easter weather,
some hours of warmth and sun.

A mind to walk in still:
in a vacated sanctuary

the land of the angels fills the space
between that rigour and the expansive fields of Autumn;
an ear of intent hunger
discerns the rustling of their feet like corn
sun-gilded, absolute and easy.
A treasury is folded
down deep inside earth's air—
broad combs of light warmed in a cloak of dust,
and the body of all gods quiescent there.

A REDUNDANT CHURCH

   The dark has been expelled.
Thorns nuzzle under crumbled plaster
  where the rood pales to a dust that volleys
     on a flare of wings

  signalling the order of release.
To stoop and enter is to step right out
  into more space than time contains
    or quiet can sing.

SOMERSBY

When dawn draws back the shade
black light will fade in amber,
from lawn and brook and cedar
the rooks unfold in flight
to pewter clouds unshining
as hands that fought repose
move into daylight, mourning.

Quiet sounds grow into sight:
the shrouded robin's song
calls Lazarus from the rose;
each flute and casual stirring
throngs to make a burial bourdon
in the heart of him who longs
to wake, to greet the unreturning.

HOLLYWOOD THE GOLDEN

Helen Kane, whose gay little girl's voice made the phrase 'boop-boop-a-doop' a part of the legend of the roaring 20's died yesterday at 62 after a 10-year battle with cancer.
—from an American newspaper

Oh, the gay girl's gone now
    further than even she could dance,
far from the inter-stellar bars
    into her ultimate romance;

she's gone out to the metropole
    where the dead stars dine,
their dreams of silk and money blessed
    in haze of Metro Goldwyn wine.

There, Great Sugar Daddy smiles
    on all his slim blonde babies,
on Carole Lombard, Thelma Todd
    and 'lovely Marion Davies'.

Where Connie Bennett pours the drinks
    Jeanette can sing for hours,
Louella still supplying news
    and Forest Lawn the flowers.

No longer do they have to pose
    or answer the reporters;
their contracts now are at an end,
    they rest by perfumed waters.

Jean Harlow finds her heart's desire,
    there's peace for Clara Bow;
and her lost childhood is restored
    to Marilyn Monroe.

And now another gay girl's gone,
    another dancing daughter:

Boop-boop-a-doop! the darling sang,
    till the cruel crab caught her.

For a brief while her face is seen:
    Boop-boop-a-doop! the headlines hymn.
Do You Remember Helen Kane?
    The Broadway lights recede and dim,

for she is gone to the Good Place
    where all the lovelies find their past
with Oscars they have never won,
    their great comeback made at last.

VERONICA

The river's sluggish here,
under the elders. I have come to rest,
    Veronica beside me,

    her face veiled with loving,
so kind it bears a blessed reflection.
    I see no likeness.

    All I have ever seen
is the garden—rosemary, lilac, espaliers
    of pear and apple—

    and the house with the child in it;
he is looking forward to meeting Veronica.
    Though plagued by witches

    he is aware there will be a river,
pollard willows and these open fields
    and the hands of Veronica

    to stroke away the fears.
Just like this: and he'll repulse them,
    held from then on

    in a bleaker landscape, gently
regarded by his own grieving for Veronica
    who cannot save him,

    whom he will never achieve,
entombed as his several ages are
    in a garden of lilacs

    the size of his own soul.
The current shivers. How shall I ever reach you
    now, Veronica?

MASTER AND SERVANT

Death wakes me in the morning,
   my loyal good friend,
attentive and to be trusted
   to what he is—the end.

My alter-ego, glass
   into which I gaze
spelling my future, granting
   depth to all my days;

guage, censor and reprieve;
   life's certain accolade;
easy as birth, the reason
   never to be afraid:

death is all these I know—
   a standard to maintain;
accepted, a sure weapon
   to arm me against pain.

But ageing too, will he
   betray this confidence
with slow decay, with agony,
   disgust, incontinence?

He will—save for a wanton
   seizure or mischance;
true always to this life I lead,
   he squares, then calls, the dance.

THE MAIDS OF LE MANS

It was a failure of power, Monsieur,
that made us do it, the inability
to complete our work; our obedience
short-circuited. Madame
with her white gloves would perceive
the dust upon them: how could we
do their will in the dark?
We are clean girls, and godly;
from our attic we can watch
the nuns and widows moving
on the pavement to the early mass.
We have scrubbed and polished carefully,
(Madame could see in the dark—
Down on your knees, girl!
She made us hate the dust.
And Mademoiselle would be her tongue,
her other eye.)
     No, Monsieur,
a good servant goes over to her enemies,
and we had to do our duty in the dark:
the ladies required it.
      But if the power,
if the light, failed, where was our duty?
We did the only thing we could:
Madame would have scolded otherwise.
So—a tooth and eye out each,
with knife and hammer to cut off the noise,
one after the other. We were accustomed
to slicing up the meat, it was no trouble;
we put everything back in its place, contrite
about the dented pewter pitcher . . .
        Monsieur?
We are ready to go: we are good girls.
We trust we have given satisfaction.

BIG BABY

    A poppet to begin with
    and when yowling cherished
  he'd bump around the house
    to collide with corners
    wielding his rattle
    like a jolly tomahawk.
  A regular jelly-baby
all squeezable under the woollies
knitted by aunt after aunt after aunt
he'd fold into every shape for loving.

    But how he grew!
    The plump thighs
  swelled to colossi staggering,
    the pink nails
    were looking glasses
    and when he hollered
  the tiles blew off the roof.
  He grew out of doors and windows;
his nappies' state disgraced the neighbourhood.
We bore with it, loving our baby boy.

    You were the first
    to be almost smothered.
  Reeking of bum powder
    you escaped to breathe
    but tottered fainting:
    I pulled you round
  with grown-up love's reminder.
  As the nursery floor collapsed
we came reluctantly to the conclusion
that the bursting house walls barred.

    He, unhurt,
    (of course) we
  bundled up therefore
    and towed strenuously
    along the street

to a policeman—
who looked confused and scowled
   hard, not at us,
but down at our infant juggernaut
gone tiny, weeping, bruised.

AT THE SPA

We should not be here, hating this mothball hush of villas,
conifers and a half-erected church (C of E).
By a decrepit bandstand we watch a Canon Missioner
be cheerful at young people as they dance.
I kiss you cautiously.

You are disturbed: the receptionist
seems disapproving. We do not play golf,
and our luggage is baggage: we are therefore an intrusion.
Ordered to order dinner in the bar please, we drink
and pay and drink and fidget; at the end too full for love.

What can these waters heal? There are rheumatics of the heart
the Princess Alice Avenue is too straight-paced to ease . . .
The manager and his mistress appear to be in drag:
they gobble down their Strogonoff till half-past ten,
keeping the waiters waiting.

We attend each other's pleasure.
Our bodies move together in the cure, the cure!
while the hotel belly-gurgles from a score of wash bowls
and hands grown itchy for the club. The morning's fine.
                                        Content
but hungry,
we are informed No Breakfast After Nine.

DODDYNELL

Going back—so you called it;
for me that may was dying.

But what do old eyes look for
when they refute compassion?

The hill meadow, Doddynell:
it was held to through the rain,

black rain cutting down the ring road
with the new grass seeding,

broken bottles and a site for sale.
You could recall the hay

(your last meal is at five) waiting
for the sun on Doddynell,

a wedding in June, the Canterbury bells;
we were going back together,

but you've outrun me: there is nowhere,
the repository of the Home,

my return journey, aching. For you,
Doddynell. And the may blossom.

As you turn back in their direction
your bent bones shape that land.

WET SLEDDALE: On Good Friday

    Dammed: not only airy waters—
       more. And drowned. The waste,
       mute with crumbled shippons,
          its shaggy grass
          untrimmed by sheep,
       holds less than silence, a suspension
    as the valley, not unborn but dead,
is scoured-out for the curlew's hollow call.

    Dun vapour: all the morning
       was a holding back, a welling
       pressure of tears, a hunger.
          Now a hunted walking
          with a twilight thirst.
       To tread through mire and thistles
    seemed a queer gesture, unavailing,
for only a bridge to nowhere marked the journey's end.

    Such mournfulness! Converging cataracts,
       slowed to a shred of stream,
       were silenced in their own excess.
          The smitten rocks
          cluttered a wilderness
       drained that we might drink.
      The valley's barricade impounds
a careless mercy struck from the hills' side,

    defines its course: the need is sure,
       arterial, absolute.
       The moors bow down;
          ducts, borings
          are channels of grace,
       constitute a propriety.
    This pack-horse bridge, considerately preserved,
brings to a halt my vague, recessional feet.

    Something is mourning here, an element
       I have touched, felt,

> drawn back from.
> I am Caesar,
> follow the roads,
> the old tracks I cover
> with my own pursuits mimicking the rest,
> haunted by absence at the thought of byre and thorn.

IN THE GARDENS: VILLA CIMBRONE

Spice hour: noon shutters close.
The bronze boy's flank
blisters the fingers;
lizards rustle
across the papery leaves,
and a bell booms.

On the belvedere the old Marchesa
cracks in the dry heat.
There's nutmeg scent
and dust in her hair:
she could tell you of Garibaldi
if you kissed her hand.

Plaster drops. Cypresses
shift in the sweet wind:
another boy,
from a winter country,
peers from two hungry
older eyes,

feeding on the chipped and flaking urn,
the pergola, the clematis
that stirs in greeting;
under the oleander
he gazes up the stairway
to an arch of blue.

On what shell-bright icy morning
glinting in the fire of frost
did the memory begin?
crackle of pine-log
prompt conception? book
give birth?

Forsaken Psyche of a northern king
or the south's immortal rose:

celestial statuary
warms to the bodies
of those stately living ladies,
mother goddesses

gliding and murmuring with fan and feather
below the colonnade
where wafts of lemon
and mimosa float
past tall Calabrian pines.
Memory, sight

blend in a quiet of stone
as dawn and twilight chime:
the angelus—
young Mary,
older than the musky cedar,
opening her arms.

The child stirs; he sees and knows;
wrapped in this light he renders
to the sundial, stopped
at a late hour,
his early adoration.
Death smiles

through the eyes of the bronze boy; complete,
the garden moves no longer,
held in air
too bright and pure
for the old black spires
across the walks

nodding in a sharp sea-breath
above the chequered vineyards . . .
The Marchesa lowers
her parasol:
footsteps and chatter move her
to take her leave.

Boys' eyes on the tossed valerian
blur, forget: alone
visible is the stricken
aristocratic
figure fading homeward
through the guardian gate.

THE BRINK

The river's solid as might be the air
that gluts my throat, that gnaws cathedral
stone beyond renewal. Low bells are shaken
   thundering on the speed of dark
      across the fen.

Can you be taken? The saint's finger
in its casket pines for resurrection.
Flesh stays cold: consign yourself
   to flame. The unbaptized
      should know their hour.

PRIESTED SHORE

In the haze of early morning
There is no limit to the sea
I am what I have not become

All is known and is not there
Nor below the sea's shining
Is the unknown fathomless

Calm as a pearl this early morning
The bread broken to my blinding
I have lost the sun at the sun's rising

RUINED

    Here the trip must end.
    Earlier, in this eastward land
      that cups the sundown
  you should have been here and were not.
Your absence was a cloud enveloping all else.

    Others at this spot had studied
    to see beyond the sun,
      steady on the object,
  time in order, all obstacles foregone.
They knew far more than I was able to desire.

    Now you are here;
    I have what I have wanted,
      movement and words
  just right, with the kindness in your body
brief and healing as the sunbeam on the stone.

    So prayers come true.
    Such grace demolishes
      my plaster temple.
  A magpie pecks about the fostered ruins
by a water slide; the lawns, with my grief, are green.

THE DISPOSAL OF THE DEAD

Grey boughs of February can fall
   like smoke about these rocks,
     a shroud of rheumy vapour
that hushes the swift passage of the Dove
       through limestone reaches.

      When will you smile?
So bent on what is over, young,
   and old now to be silly,
     you move in anger, swung
on your shouldering way through cleft and thicket.

The gorge flattens to a backdrop framed
   as I remembered. If anywhere
     it's someone's picture on a wall
that now I stare hard out of, flinching
       through a veil of branches

      from the cold summons
of a morgue. The dead are stacked and waiting
   tallow-coloured on the ice;
     her hands that tipped the picture—
see, the hill-slope tilts—have foundered.

Her survivor toils in fever, clutching
   death, and frantic in pursuit:
     I tread behind you so,
the stir of him a trouble in my blood
       that longs to hold you,

      young one, close
on this green bank where the friendly fisherman
   would heal and feed his thousands.
     O, good uncle death
should salt our feast with grateful tears

for what came after and by now is gone!
    The valley of the shadow opening
    as we draw near each other
changes time: your wide eyes,
       grey as smoke

       upon these rocks,
hold every prospect since they spell
    our past. So frown, if you must,
    in the cloud that held me dead
and waking; your smile is in my will.

MINE

    Black quiet
and a barred door:

    this cell
warms its keeper

    reborn
from life's sentence,

    dumb from
recovered breath.

God of the rock
    spare me

such little room
    cleared out

of hard-won clay.
    No word

now from the past,
    just this

clear calling day.